Fantastic Fondue R

A Complete Cookbook of Delicious Dipping Ideas!

BY: Allie Allen

COOK & ENJOY

Cheesy Pumpkin Fondue 43

Decadent Crab Fondue 46

Mushroom & Ham Fondue 49

German-Style Broth & Steak Fondue 52

Chili Queso Fondue 54

Wine & Veal Fondue 57

Cherry Brandy & Cheese Fondue 59

Veggie Stock Fondue 61

Garlic & Oil Fondue 63

Beefy Broth Fondue 65

Bourbon Cheese Fondue 67

Dessert Fondue Recipes 70

White Chocolate Fondue 71

Cheesecake Fondue 73

Cocoa & Chocolate Fondue 75

Strawberry Fondue 77

Peanut Butter Fondue 79

Conclusion 81

About the Author.. 82

Author's Afterthoughts.. 84

Introduction

Where did fondue originate?

How can you include the tastiest cheeses, broths, and chocolates in your fondue dishes?

Why is a fondue dinner so much more user-friendly than traditional meals?

Although the term "fondue" comes from the French word for "melt", is actually was first enjoyed in Sweden in the early 18th century. Fondue dinners are easy to prepare and served in traditional pots made from earthenware. The pots retain heat and distribute it evenly.

Usually, diners use long forks, spearing cubes of bread, meat, veggies or fruits, which are dipped in cheese, broth, oil, or, for dessert, chocolate. You can get creative with the utensils, as long as they are long and can handle the heat.

For the simplest fondue, bread cubes and cheese, eating is a delicious experience. You just spear a bread cube with a fork, then dip it in the pot. Twirl the cube of bread gently in cheese, coating it, then allow the bread to drip a little before you nibble or gobble the cheese coated bread – careful, it's hot! Be sure you don't touch your lips or your tongue to the fork since that fork will be in the fondue pot again.

Whether you are serving cheese, oil, broth, or chocolate or butterscotch for dessert dishes, you're in for a fun time and great taste. Enjoy preparing and serving a fondue soon!

Fondue Recipes for Lunch, Dinner, Snacks & Appetizers

Gruyere Cheese & Wine Fondue

This recipe offers the tantalizing taste of cheese made more interesting by the addition of wine. It has a taste all your friends will love when they dip bread chunks in it.

Makes 5 Servings

Cooking + Prep Time: 25 minutes

Ingredients:

- 1 cup of wine, dry white
- 1/2 lb. of Gruyere cheese shreds
- 1/2 lb. of Swiss cheese shreds
- 2 tbsp. of flour, all-purpose
- 1/4 tsp. of salt, kosher
- 1/4 tsp. of nutmeg, ground
- 1 x 1-lb. loaf of cubed bread, French

Instructions:

1. Simmer the wine in your fondue pot.

2. Add cheeses, 1/4 lb. after another. Stir following every addition till cheese melts. Add flour and stir well. When all cheese melts, add salt & nutmeg and stir.

3. Dip cubes of French bread in cheese to serve and share.

Pancetta & Onion Fondue

This fondue is based on pancetta and Gouda cheese spiced with cumin. You can serve it with pickled veggies or soft pretzels for dipping enjoyment.

Makes 8 Servings

Cooking + Prep Time: 45 minutes

Ingredients:

- 4 ounces of pancetta, sliced thickly
- 1 onion, red, sliced
- 1 tsp. of cumin, ground
- Salt, kosher
- Pepper, ground
- 1 pound of Gouda cheese
- 2 tbsp. of flour, all-purpose
- 3/4 cup of Riesling, dry

For dipping

- 8 pretzels, soft
- Cubed bread
- Pickled veggies

Instructions:

1. In a medium-sized skillet, cook pancetta on med-high, while occasionally stirring, for six to eight minutes, till crisp. Transfer pancetta to plate. Pour off all fat except 1 tbsp. from skillet.

2. Add sliced onion and cover the skillet. Cook on medium heat for five or six minutes, till they soften. Add 2 tbsp. water to skillet. Stir occasionally while cooking till onion browns lightly, five more minutes. Stir in cumin. Season onions as desired.

3. Toss flour and cheese in a mixing bowl. In a medium pan, bring wine to simmer on medium heat. Add cheese slowly in handfuls and constantly stir till every batch melts completely, before you add more cheese.

4. Stir vigorously while cooking for a couple minutes till mixture is creamy. Stir in 1/2 of onions and the pancetta. Generously season using ground pepper. Float remainder of onion slices atop fondue. Transfer to fondue pot and serve with dippers.

French Onion Fondue

French onion-filled fondue is better than soup since it's creamier, thicker, and richer. It's even simpler to make, and you can dip many different things in it.

Various # of Servings

Cooking + Prep Time: 55 minutes

Ingredients:

- 4 cups of Gruyere cheese shreds
- 1 tbsp. of cornstarch
- 2 tsp. of chopped thyme, fresh
- 1 tbsp. of butter, unsalted
- 1 tbsp. of oil, olive
- 5 cups of onion, sliced thinly
- 1 cup of beef broth, low sodium
- Salt, kosher, as desired
- Pepper, ground, as desired
- 3/4 cup of sherry, dry
- 1/4 cup of white wine, dry

For dipping

- Celery stalks
- Broccoli
- Bread cubes
- Tortilla chips

Instructions:

1. Cut a piece of parchment paper into a circle of about the diameter of a large pan. Cut circular 2-inch vent in the middle.

2. Toss cheese, thyme and corn starch together.

3. Melt the butter and oil in large pan on med-high.

4. Add broth and onions and season as desired. Cook till broth has almost evaporated, 12-15 minutes or so. Cover onions with the parchment circle made above. Reduce the heat level to med-low. Continue to cook till onions are deeply golden brown, while occasionally stirring. This usually takes about a half-hour. Transfer the onions to a bowl. Increase the heat up to med.

5. Deglaze the pan using wine and sherry. Scrape up browned bits from sides and bottom. Bring mixture to simmer. Whisk in the cheese mixture one handful after another, allowing each handful to melt fully before you add another.

6. Add and stir in the onions. Season as desired. Transfer mixture to heated fondue pot. Serve with dippers.

Pizza Fondue

Pizza parlors have nothing over this fondue style pizza. It's best when you serve it with crackers or breadsticks

For dipping.

Makes 6-8 Servings

Cooking + Prep

Time:1/2 hour

Carbs:

- 2 cups of mozzarella shreds + extra to top
- 1/3 cup of Parmesan cheese, freshly grated
- 1 jar of marinara sauce, organic
- 1/4 tsp. of oregano, dried
- 1 pkg. of pepperoni mini's

For dipping

- Crackers
- Breadsticks

Instructions:

1. Pour the marinara sauce, cheeses, oregano, and handful of pepperoni mini's into your fondue pot.

2. Heat till cheeses melt and stir, combining well.

3. Top with extra mozzarella & pepperoni minis and serve with dippers.

Garlic Pesto Fondue

Pesto makes a simply wonderful sauce

For dipping. When added to a fondue dish, it brings forth herby-cheesy goodness that will keep guests coming back for more.

Makes 4 Servings

Cooking + Prep

Time:35 minutes

Carbs:

- 1 cup of shredded cheese, Parmesan
- 3 cups of shredded cheese, mozzarella
- 1 & 1/2 cups of wine, dry white
- 2 tbsp. of corn starch
- 3 cloves of garlic
- 1/2 cup of chopped basil leaves, fresh
- 1/4 cup of toasted almonds, walnuts or pine nuts
- Pepper, ground, as desired

For dipping

- Cauliflower florets
- Steamed broccoli florets
- Carrot sticks
- Celery sticks
- Cubed bread, baguette
- Tomatoes, cherry
- Mushrooms, sliced

Instructions:

1. Place garlic, basil and nuts in a food processor. Blend while adding 1/4 cup wine. Blend till thick and set mixture aside.

2. In a large pan, add the remainder of wine and pesto mixture. Heat till it has reached a gentle boil.

3. In a large mixing bowl, toss cheeses and corn starch. Stir slowly into pan one handful after another. Stir while cooking on med. heat till stringy and melted. This usually takes four to six minutes. Season as desired.

4. Transfer mixture to fondue pot. Use burner to keep it warm. Serve promptly with dippers.

Fireball Whiskey Fondue

This is basically an adults-only fondue since whiskey and hot sauce are featured prominently. You can make it without the whiskey and cut back on the hot sauce if you have children coming to your fondue party.

Makes 12 Servings

Cooking + Prep

Time: 35 minutes

Carbs:

- 1 & 1/2 cups of cheddar cheese, grated
- 1 & 1/2 cups of cheddar cheese, white, grated
- 2 tbsp. of corn starch
- 1 cup of lager, light
- 2 tbsp. of whiskey, Fireball®
- 1 tbsp. of hot sauce – Tabasco, etc.

For dipping

- Bread cubes
- Vegetables

Instructions:

1. In a medium-sized bowl, toss the cheeses and corn starch together.

2. In a pan on med. heat, add the lager. Bring to simmer. Add cheese mixture gradually and whisk, combining well.

3. Stir in the hot sauce and whiskey. Season as desired. Stir frequently till mixture bubbles.

4. Transfer to fondue pot with heat source. Serve with your choice of dippers.

Gruyere & Shallot Fondue

The white wine and Gruyere cheese in this recipe are balanced nicely by caramelized shallots. Cheese should be added in small, slow batches, so the fondue will be very creamy.

Makes 8 Servings

Cooking + Prep

Time: 40 minutes

Carbs:

- 6 oz. of shallots, sliced thinly
- 1 tbsp. of butter, unsalted
- 1 tsp. of sugar, granulated
- 1 tsp. of salt, kosher
- 14 oz. of Gruyere cheese, grated finely
- 2 tbsp. of flour, all-purpose
- 1 & 1/2 cups of wine, dry white
- A pinch of nutmeg, ground (generously-sized)
- 1 minced garlic clove, small
- 2 tbsp. of brandy, apple, like Calvados or similar
- A generous amount of pepper, ground

For dipping

- White bread cubes
- Sliced sausage
- Mushrooms
- Broccoli florets
- Apple slices

Instructions:

1. Melt the butter on med. heat in heavy pan. Add the shallots. Cook for two minutes. Then add granulated sugar and kosher salt. Stir occasionally while cooking for 12-16 minutes.

2. As shallots caramelize, grate cheese. Add to large mixing bowl. Toss with flour.

3. Add wine to shallots. Bring to boil for one minute. Add cheese slowly, one handful after another. Make sure cheese melts and pot has returned to boil before you add the next handful. Continue till you have added all cheese and all has melted.

4. Add and whisk in garlic, nutmeg, ground pepper and brandy. Season as desired. Transfer to fondue pot with candle warming it and serve with dippers.

Smoky Mozzarella Italian-Style Fondue

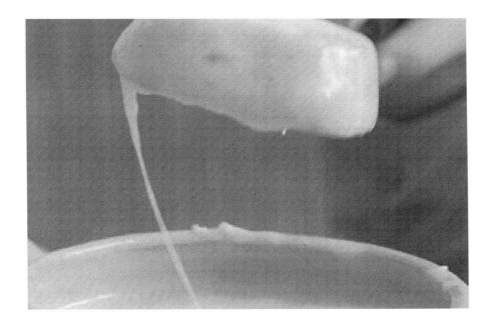

This was not an original recipe but rather was inspired by an Olive Garden™ dish. I have tweaked it though, and you may like it more than the original.

Makes 6-8 Servings

Cooking + Prep

Time: 35 minutes

Carbs:

- 8 ounces of softened cream cheese, reduced fat
- 1 cup of mozzarella cheese, smoked
- 1 cup of cheese, provolone
- 1/2 cup of Parmesan cheese, freshly grated
- 1/3 cup of sour cream, low fat
- 1/2 tsp. of thyme, dried
- 1/2 tsp. of seasoning blend, Italian
- 1/4 tsp. of pepper flakes, red
- Salt, kosher
- Pepper, ground
- 1 chopped tomato, small
- 1 tbsp. of chopped parsley, fresh

For dipping

Baguette bread, cubed

Instructions:

1. Preheat the oven to 350F.

2. In a large mixing bowl, combine the cheese, cream cheese, thyme, sour cream, pepper flakes and Italian seasoning blend. Stir well till combined fully and smooth. Season as desired.

3. Transfer cheese to a small-sized skillet. Cook for about 20 to 25 minutes till it bubbles.

4. Transfer cheese again to fondue pot with heat source under it. Keep warm. Use parsley and tomatoes to garnish. Serve with cubed bread.

Stout Ale & Irish Cheddar Fondue

This dish, although meatless, is very rich and flavorful. It makes a wonderful appetizer for carry-in dinners.

Makes 6 Servings

Cooking + Prep

Time: 50 minutes

Carbs:

- 2 cups of halved and 1"-cubed potatoes, red-skinned
- 2 cups of florets, cauliflower
- 2 cups of brussels sprouts, small
- 2 cored, wedge-cut apples, fresh
- 1 lb. of grated cheddar, Irish – you can substitute sharp white cheddar
- 2 & 1/2 tbsp. of flour, all-purpose
- 3/4 cup of Guinness or other stout, Irish
- 6 tbsp. of frozen/thawed juice concentrate, apple
- 1 tbsp. of mustard, Dijon

Instructions:

1. Steam the veggies till they are tender, 12-15 minutes or so. Arrange apples and vegetables around large platter edge.

2. Toss flour and cheese in a large mixing bowl.

3. Bring the Guinness, mustard and apple juice concentrate to a simmer in a large pan on med. heat. Add cheese mixture gradually, while constantly stirring, till cheese is smooth and melted. Season as desired.

4. Transfer mixture to fondue pot on a large platter. Serve with veggies.

Cheddar Veggie Fondue

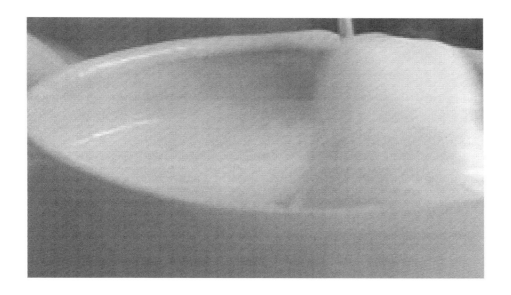

This wonderful-tasting fondue is a perennial favorite in our home. We serve it with all kinds of veggies, like broccoli, squash, zucchini, celery, and more.

Makes 4 Servings

Cooking + Prep

Time: 20 minutes

Carbs:

- 4 cups of cheddar cheese shreds
- 1 tbsp. of flour, all-purpose
- 1 cup of beer, non-alcoholic if you have kids sharing
- 3 minced cloves of garlic
- 1 & 1/2 tsp. of mustard, ground
- 1/4 tsp. of pepper, ground coarsely

For dipping

- Carrot sticks
- Mushrooms
- Broccoli florets
- Squash
- Radishes
- Zucchini
- Celery sticks

Instructions:

1. In a large mixing bowl, combine cheddar shreds and flour.

2. Heat beer, mustard, garlic & ground pepper in small pan on med. heat till you see bubbles forming on pan sides.

3. Reduce the heat level to med-low. Add one handful cheese mixture. While stirring constantly, cook till cheese has nearly finished melting. Continue to add cheese mixture, one handful after another, letting cheese melt almost completely before your next addition.

4. Transfer to fondue pot with heat source. Keep fondue warm and serve with dippers.

Cider & Cheese Fondue

This fondue has an interesting and delicious flavor, brought about by the apple brandy, hard cider, and cider vinegar.

For dipping, we like to use bread cubes, kielbasa, and apples.

Makes 4-6 Servings

Cooking + Prep

Time: 50 minutes

Carbs:

- 4 cups of Gruyere cheese, grated coarsely
- 1 tbsp. + 2 tsp. of corn starch
- 1 cup of apple cider, hard
- 1 tbsp. of vinegar, apple cider
- 2 tbsp. of Calvados or other brandy, apple

For dipping

- 2 cored & 1/2"-sliced apples, Granny Smith if available
- 8 oz. of 1/2"-sliced sausage, kielbasa
- 1 x 3/4" cubed baguette loaf

Instructions:

1. Preheat the oven to 300F.

2. Heat a large, heavy skillet on high. Add slices of kielbasa. Sauté till both sides have browned, two to three minutes. Transfer to cookie sheet. Place in 300F oven and keep them warm.

3. Toss corn starch and cheese in a large mixing bowl, coating the cheese well.

4. Bring the vinegar and hard cider to simmer in a pan on med. heat. Reduce the heat level to med-low to keep mixture simmering just barely.

5. Add one handful of Gruyere cheese to the simmering mixture. Stir till cheese melts. Add the remainder of cheese one handful after another and stir after each addition till cheese melts.

6. Raise heat level to medium. Stir constantly while cooking till fondue has started bubbling. Stir in the apple brandy. Season as desired.

7. Transfer mixture to fondue pot with lit candle under it. Arrange cubed bread, sliced sausage and sliced apples in separate bowls by the pot and serve.

Zesty Mexican Fondue

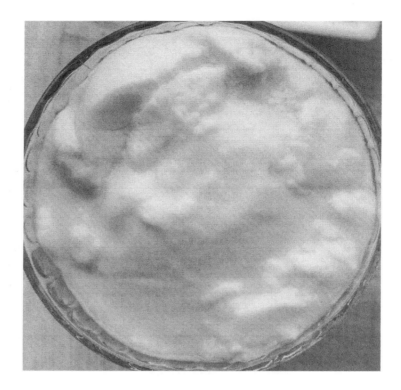

This dish comes together quickly, with a short list of ingredients and just a bit of preparation. Your slow cooker does most of the work for you.

Makes 5 Servings

Cooking + Prep

Time: 1 hour & 45 minutes

Carbs:

- 1 x 14 & 3/4-oz. can of corn, cream-style
- 1 x 14 & 1/2-oz. can of drained tomatoes, diced
- 3 tbsp. of green chilies, chopped
- 1 x 16-oz. pkg. of cubed cheese, Velveeta®
- 1 tsp. of chili powder, +/- as desired

For dipping

- Cubed French bread

Instructions:

1. In a small-sized bowl, combine corn, chilies, tomatoes & chili powder. Add cheese and stir well.

2. Pour the cheese mixture in a small slow cooker. Cover. Cook on the high setting till cheese melts, stirring every 1/2 hour for 1 & 1/2 hours.

3. Transfer mixture to fondue pot. Serve with cubed bread for dipping.

Oka Cheese & Wine Fondue

Oka cheese is a semi-soft cheese made in Canada. It's named after the town where it was first made. You can substitute another semi-soft cheese if you can't find oka cheese locally.

Makes 8-10 Servings

Cooking + Prep

Time: 35 minutes

Carbs:

- 1 & 1/4 cups of cream, heavy
- 1/2 cup of wine, dry white
- 1/2 cup of wine, ice
- 3 tbsp. of flour, all-purpose
- 1 pound of cheese, Oka if available – remove the rind and grate coarsely

For dipping

- Baguette, cubed
- Wedge-cut pears
- Wedge-cut apples

Instructions:

1. Whisk wines, cream & flour together in a heavy pan till you have a smooth mixture. Bring to boil on med. heat while constantly stirring, till silky and thickened, four to six minutes.

2. Add 1/2 of the cheese. Gently stir till nearly melted. Add the remainder of cheese. Cook and stir till cheese has melted and mixture has a smooth texture, two to four minutes. Transfer to heated fondue pot and serve with dippers.

Party-Ready Fondue

We have parties fairly often, and fondues are always a hit. For dipping, we often use vegetables, pears, apples, and cubes of bread.

Makes 3 Servings

Cooking + Prep

Time: 25 minutes

Carbs:

- 1/2 cup of Swiss cheese shreds
- 2 cups of Jarlsberg cheese shreds – add extra 2 cups of Swiss if you can't find Jarlsberg cheese
- 1/4 cup of flour, all-purpose
- 1/2 tsp. of mustard, ground
- 1/2 tsp. of pepper, ground
- 1 cup of whipping cream, heavy
- 1 cup chicken broth, reduced sodium
- 1 tbsp. of honey, pure
- 1 tsp. of lemon juice, fresh

For dipping

- Assorted veggies
- Sliced apples
- Spiced pears
- French bread, cubed

Instructions:

1. In a small mixing bowl, add the first five ingredients and toss, combining well.

2. In a medium pan, combine the broth, cream and honey. Bring barely to boil while occasionally stirring. Reduce the heat level to med-low. Add 1/2 cup of the cheese mixture made in step 1, stirring constantly till nearly melted.

3. Continue to add cheese by half cups full and allow each addition to melt almost fully before adding more. Stir till mixture is smooth and thickened. Add lemon juice and stir.

4. Transfer the mixture to pre-heated fondue pot and keep it gently bubbling. Serve with veggies, fruits and bread cubes for dipping.

Cheesy Pumpkin Fondue

In this recipe, the pumpkin is roasted and the skin becomes burnished. Inside, cheese and baguette slices create a velvety, rich combination that is simply fabulous.

Makes 8 Servings

Cooking + Prep

Time: 1 hour & 55 minutes

Carbs:

- 1 x 7-8-lb. pumpkin, orange
- 1 & 1/2 cups of cream, heavy
- 1 cup of vegetable broth, low sodium
- 1/2 tsp. of nutmeg, grated
- 2 & 1/2 cups of Gruyere cheese, grated coarsely
- 2 & 1/2 cups of Emmental cheese, grated coarsely
- 1 tbsp. of oil, olive

For dipping

- 1 x 15" baguette piece, cut in 1/2" slices

Instructions:

1. Place rack in the lower 1/3 of oven. Preheat to 450F.

2. Place slices of baguette on cookie sheet. Put in the oven till bread is still pale but tops have become crispy. Transfer to rack and allow them to cool.

3. Remove pumpkin top. Cut 3" diameter circle around the stem. Scrape out fibers and seeds from pumpkin. Season inside pumpkin using 1/2 tsp. of kosher salt.

4. Whisk broth, cream, nutmeg, 1 tsp. of salt & 1/2 tsp. of pepper together in a medium bowl. Mix cheeses together in separate bowl.

5. Place layer of crisped bread in the bottom of your pumpkin. Cover with a cup of cheese and 1/2 cup of the cream mixture. Then continue layering the bread, then cheese, then cream mixture till the pumpkin is filled about 1/2" from the top.

6. Cover the pumpkin with its top. Set in small-sized roasting pan. Brush outside using olive oil. Then bake in 450F oven till pumpkin becomes tender & the filling has puffed up, 1 & 1/4 – 1 & 1/2 hours. Serve with the pumpkin as your fondue pot.

Decadent Crab Fondue

When I want to impress guests, even at a relaxed fondue party, I reach for this recipe. The crab meat makes them feel like I'm indulging them and welcoming them to our table.

Makes 8 Servings

Cooking + Prep

Time: 35 minutes

Carbs:

- 1/2 cup of cubed butter, unsalted
- 3 chopped onions, green
- 2 x 8-oz. pkgs. of chopped crab meat, real or imitation
- 2 cups of milk, whole
- 1/2 cup of chicken broth, reduced sodium
- 1/4 tsp. of pepper, ground
- 2 cups of Monterey Jack shreds
- 2 cups of Swiss cheese shreds
- 2 cups of Gruyere cheese shreds – you can sub more Swiss cheese here if you like
- 1 cup of Velveeta® cheese, cubed

For dipping

- French bread cubes

Instructions:

1. In a large stock pot, cook the butter on med-high. Add the onions. Stir while cooking till they become tender. Add the crab meat. Cook for two to three more minutes, till it is heated fully through.

2. Add and stir in the broth, milk and ground pepper. Heat till there are bubbles forming around pan sides.

3. Reduce the heat level to med-low. Add 1/2 cup of Monterey Jack shreds and stir till they have nearly finished melting. Continue to add all cheeses, 1/2 cup after another, making sure each amount almost melts before you add more. Stir and cook till mixture thickens, with a smooth texture.

4. Transfer the mixture to fondue pot over heat. Keep it gently bubbling. Serve with cubed bread.

Mushroom & Ham Fondue

Gruyere cheese and mushrooms add a wonderful taste to this fondue recipe. It's been a favorite in our house for years.

Makes 6 Servings

Cooking + Prep

Time: 1 hour & 5 minutes

Carbs:

- 1 cup of water, hot
- 1 oz. of dried mushrooms, porcini
- 1 minced clove of garlic
- 1 tbsp. + 1 & 1/4 cups of wine, dry white
- 2 tsp. of corn starch
- 8 oz. of Gruyere cheese, grated coarsely
- 8 oz. of Emmental cheese, grated coarsely

For dipping

- 2 lbs. of 1/4" thick slices of ham, cut in 1" pieces
- 1 x 1-lb. of 1" cubed bread, ciabatta

Instructions:

1. Place a cup of heated water in a small mixing bowl. Add dried mushrooms. Allow to stand for 20-25 minutes, till mushrooms have become soft. Remove and chop finely.

2. Transfer the soaking liquid into large-sized skillet. Leave sediment in a bowl. Add mushrooms and garlic. Simmer on med. heat till nearly all the liquid has been absorbed, three to five minutes. Season as desired.

3. Place the fondue pot on stand. Light Sterno or candle.

4. Mix 1 tbsp. of wine with corn starch in a small-sized bowl. Bring last 1 & 1/4 cups of wine to a simmer in large, heavy pan on med-high.

5. Add cheese in small-sized handfuls and stir till it melts. Add the corn starch mixture and bring to a simmer. Stir till the fondue has thickened a bit and has begun bubbling, one or two minutes. Season as desired.

6. Pour the mixture in the prepared fondue pot. Swirl in mushrooms. Serve with dippers.

German-Style Broth & Steak Fondue

This recipe lets you cook and enjoy a meal together with friends or family (or both). It can also be used for a romantic dinner.

Makes 4 Servings

Cooking + Prep

Time: 55 minutes

Carbs:

- 4 cups of beef broth, low sodium
- 1 cup of wine, white
- 3 sliced onions, green
- 3 minced garlic cloves

For dipping

- Steak cubes
- Broccoli florets
- Cauliflower florets
- Mushrooms

Instructions:

1. Heat broth, wine, garlic and green onions in a pan on med. heat till the mixture boils. Reduce heat to simmer.

2. Slice meat in cubes and vegetables in small florets.

3. Transfer broth fondue to your fondue pot with heat source under it. Serve and cook steak and veggies by dipping and holding in broth. They take about five minutes per chunk to cook.

Chili Queso Fondue

This chili queso fondue is quite the treat and a favorite at parties. It can be kept warm in your fondue pot or a skillet.

Makes 6-8 Servings

Cooking + Prep

Time: 55 minutes

Carbs:

- 1 chopped tomato, small
- 1 seeded & chopped chile, serrano
- 2 tbsp. of chopped oregano, fresh
- Salt, kosher
- 8 oz. of mild cheddar, grated coarsely
- 8 oz. of Monterey Jack cheese, grated coarsely
- 1 tbsp. of flour, all-purpose
- 1 x 4-oz. link of Italian hot sausage or chorizo – remove the casing
- 1/2 cup of onion, minced
- 1/2 cup of lager, light

For dipping

- Tortilla chips

Instructions:

1. Mix the chile, tomatoes and oregano in a small mixing bowl. Season using kosher salt, as desired. Allow this salsa to sit for 1/2 hour

2. Toss cheeses and flour together in medium-sized bowl. Cook the chorizo in pan on med. heat, breaking it up as it cooks till it starts to render, one minute or so. Add the onions. Continue to cook till chorizo has cooked through and the onions are translucent and soft, five minutes.

3. Transfer the chorizo mixture to a small-sized bowl and return pan to medium heat. Add the lager. Stir occasionally while simmering and scrape up browned bits, if any.

4. Add the cheese mixture 1/4-cup after another while constantly whisking. Make sure the mixture is smooth and blended well before you add more cheese. Stir in the chorizo mixture and combine.

5. Spoon the salsa over chile queso. Serve in fondue pot or skillet with chips.

Wine & Veal Fondue

This is a wonderful, wine-kissed fondue, in which you can cook veal, as I did here, or chicken or even rabbit. It's so easy to cook the bite-sized raw meat pieces in the fondue pot.

Makes 4 Servings

Cooking + Prep

Time: 1 & 1/4 hour

Carbs:

- 1 bottle of wine, white
- 1 x 2" piece of stick-type cinnamon
- 1/4 tsp. of coriander, ground
- 10 crushed peppercorns, black
- 4 cloves, whole
- 1 tsp. of sugar, granulated
- 1 tsp. of salt, kosher
- 1 tsp. of salt, celery
- 1/4 tsp. of salt, garlic

For dipping

- Raw pieces of veal, rabbit or chicken

Instructions:

1. Pour the wine in a pan. Season using partial cinnamon stick, pepper, coriander, cloves, salt, sugar, garlic salt & celery salt. Allow to sit for an hour. Bring to boil.

2. Filter mixture through cheesecloth-lined colander. Transfer to fondue pan over heat. Bring to boil. Cook the meat bites in the heated broth.

Cherry Brandy & Cheese Fondue

Swiss fondue often includes cherry brandy. It adds a wonderful flavor to the already delicious melty Swiss cheese.

Makes 6 Servings

Cooking + Prep

Time: 35 minutes

Carbs:

- 1 crosswise-halved clove of garlic
- 1 & 1/2 cups of white wine, dry
- 1 tbsp. of corn starch
- 2 tsp. of brandy, cherry
- 1/2 pound of coarsely grated Gruyere cheese
- 1/2 pound of coarsely grated Emmental cheese

For dipping

- French bread cubes

Instructions:

1. Rub the inside of heavy, large pot using cut garlic clove sides. Discard the garlic. Add the wine. Bring barely to simmer on medium heat.

2. Stir brandy and corn starch together in a medium cup.

3. Add cheese gradually to large pot. Stir constantly while cooking, so cheese won't ball up. Stir till cheese is creamy and barely melted. Don't allow the mixture to boil.

4. Stir the corn starch mixture once more, then add to a pot and stir. Bring fondue mixture to simmer. Stir while cooking till mixture thickens, five to eight minutes.

5. Transfer mixture to fondue over flame. Serve with the bread to dip.

Veggie Stock Fondue

This fondue is perfect for an intimate dinner for just two. It's such a tasty dish that you probably won't have any leftovers at all.

Makes 2 Servings

Cooking + Prep

Time: 1/2 hour

Carbs:

- 3 & 1/2 cups of vegetable stock, low sodium
- 1/2 cup of wine, dry red
- 1/2 cup of sliced mushrooms, fresh
- 2 sliced onions, green
- 2 minced garlic cloves

For dipping

- Bread cubes
- Cheese cubes
- Vegetables, your choice, cut bite-sized

Instructions:

1. Heat the stock in fondue pot till it simmers. Add the wine, garlic, mushrooms and green onions. Simmer till aromatic, 13-15 minutes. Serve with dippers.

Garlic & Oil Fondue

This classic fondue dish with hot, garlicky oil is served often during the holidays in Italy. The vegetables make a healthy choice for dipping.

Makes 6 Servings

Cooking + Prep

Time: 1/2 hour

Carbs:

- 6 tbsp. of softened butter, unsalted
- 3/4 cup of oil, olive
- 12 filets of anchovy
- 6 chopped cloves of garlic, large

For dipping

- Fresh vegetables, assorted, cut in small pieces
- 1 x 1-lb. loaf of 2" cubed bread, French or Italian

Instructions:

1. Blend the butter, oil, garlic and anchovies in food processor till smooth. Transfer to a medium, heavy pan. Cook on low heat for 12-16 minutes, occasionally stirring. The sauce should separate. Season as desired.

2. Pour the sauce into a fondue pot over candle or table burner so it stays warm. Serve with bread and veggies for dipping.

Beefy Broth Fondue

Many traditional fondue recipes are based on cheese, but some are oil-based and broth-based, too. This broth-y treat allows you to dip thin vegetable or meat slices.

Makes 6 Servings

Cooking + Prep

Time: 25 minutes

Carbs:

- For the fondue mixture
- 32 ounces of beef broth, low sodium
- 1 halved garlic head
- 1/2 cup of water, filtered
- 1 tbsp. of soy sauce, reduced sodium
- 1 bay leaf, medium
- 1 tsp. of pepper, black, ground

For dipping (suggestions – you won't need all of these)

- 1 pound of beef sirloin, sliced thinly
- 1/2 pound of peeled, deveined shrimp, raw
- 1 cup of sliced mushrooms
- 1 cup of sliced carrots
- 1 cup of sliced potatoes
- 1 sliced zucchini

Instructions:

1. Combine water, broth, soy sauce, garlic, ground pepper and bay leaf in fondue pot. Bring to simmer.

2. Dip the meat, shrimp or veggies into hot broth till cooked fully through.

Bourbon Cheese Fondue

This recipe uses Babybel and Gruyere cheeses to create a tempting fondue sauce. It's sure to be a hit with your family and friends.

Makes 4 Servings

Cooking + Prep

Time: 40 minutes

Carbs:

- 2 lengthwise-halved cloves of garlic
- 1/2 cup of beer, Belgian
- 2 cups of wine, dry white
- 3 tbsp. of corn starch
- 1 lb. of coarsely grated Gruyere cheese
- 1 lb. of grated Babybel cheese
- 2 tbsp. of brandy or bourbon
- 1/4 tsp. of baking soda, pure
- 1 tbsp. of lemon juice, fresh
- Salt, kosher

For dipping

- 1"-cubed bread, country style, day-old works best
- Pickles
- Salami
- Ham

Instructions:

1. Rub the inside of a large pan with cut garlic sides. Grate the garlic finely into pan. Add 1 & 1/2 cups of wine and the beer. Bring to boil on med. heat.

2. Whisk the remainder of wine and corn starch in a small bowl till it has no lumps. Whisk mixture into the liquid in pan.

3. Bring to boil while constantly whisking. Reduce the heat till mixture is simmering gently. Add cheese gradually and whisk till smooth. Make sure each addition of cheese has been incorporated into mixture before you add more.

4. Whisk the bourbon or brandy and baking soda in a small mixing bowl. Combine well. Whisk the mixture into a pan of fondue. Add lemon juice and season as desired.

5. Transfer mixture to fondue pot with candle or Sterno to keep it warm. Serve with dippers.

Dessert Fondue Recipes

White Chocolate Fondue

There are lots of milk and dark chocolate fondue recipes, but this one uses white chocolate, with its special, sweet taste. It's easy to make with delicious dippers.

Makes 8 Servings

Cooking + Prep

Time: 10 minutes

Carbs:

- 1 x 11-oz. pkg. of white chocolate, chopped OR chocolate chips, white
- 1/4 cup of milk, 2%

For dipping

- Pretzel rods
- Mango slices
- Pineapple cubes
- Dried cherries

Instructions:

1. Combine milk and white chocolate in double boiler over gently simmering, filtered water. Stir mixture till chocolate melts.

2. Transfer mixture to fondue pot. Light candle under pot to keep mixture warm. Surround the pot with fruits and pretzels for dipping.

Cheesecake Fondue

Fondue lovers and cheesecake lovers alike will enjoy this original fondue. It goes perfectly with so many of your favorite types of dippers. It's a great holiday treat, too!

Makes 8 Servings

Cooking + Prep

Time: 15 minutes

Carbs:

- 1 x 8-ounce package of softened cream cheese, light
- 2 tbsp. of milk, whole
- 1 jar of marshmallow creme
- 1 tsp. of lemon juice, fresh

For dipping:

- Kiwi slices
- Strawberry slices
- Maraschino cherries

Instructions:

1. In a pan on med-low, combine the marshmallow cream with cream cheese. Whisk constantly while cooking till mixture melts. Be sure to pay close attention, so the mixture doesn't become scorched.

2. Add milk slowly, 1 tbsp. after another, and stir, combining well. Add lemon juice and stir it in. Combine full mixture well.

3. Remove fondue mixture from the heat. Promptly transfer to a fondue pot with candle flame burning under it. Use dipping ingredients to share.

Cocoa & Chocolate Fondue

This yummy, classic fondue adds a special twist to any get-together or party. Your friends will love dipping and sharing the treats with you.

Makes 6 Servings

Cooking + Prep

Time: 25 minutes

Carbs:

- 1/2 cup of water, filtered
- 1/2 cup of cocoa powder, unsweetened
- 1 cup of milk, 2%
- 1/4 cup of sugar, granulated
- 2 x 12-oz. bags of chocolate chips, semisweet
- 1 tsp. of vanilla extract, pure

For dipping

- Marshmallows
- Pretzels
- Cored, sliced apples
- Dried apricots

Instructions:

1. In a medium pan, combine 1/2 cup of filtered water with cocoa powder. Cook on low and stir constantly for about a minute.

2. Stir in milk & sugar & bring to simmer. Add vanilla and chocolate chips. Stir while cooking till chocolate has melted & mixture has a smooth texture, five minutes or so.

3. Serve in fondue pot with candle burning under it. Share marshmallows, pretzels, apples and apricots to dip.

Strawberry Fondue

This recipe is so simple, I was surprised that it took me as long to try as it did. It's delicious and only needs several ingredients. You can use all kinds of things

For dipping, too.

Makes Various # of Servings

Cooking + Prep

Time: 20 minutes

Carbs:

- 23 ounces of strawberries, frozen, plus sugar
- 2 tbsp. of cherry juice, maraschino
- 2 tsp. of corn starch
- 1 tbsp. of filtered water, cold

For dipping

- Angel food cake cubes
- Mandarin orange slices
- Banana slices

Instructions:

1. Place the strawberries in the food processor and mix till they are pureed. Transfer the berries to a medium pan.

2. Combine water and corn starch. Stir it into strawberry mixture.

3. Bring to boil. Then stir while cooking for a couple minutes till mixture thickens. Add cherry juice and stir well.

4. Transfer mixture to fondue pot with lit candle underneath. Use dipping ingredients to serve.

Peanut Butter Fondue

This fondue recipe has worked wonderfully for us at parties. If you have any dipping mixture leftover (don't count on it), you can use it for dessert sandwiches.

Makes 6 Servings

Cooking + Prep

Time: 25 minutes

Carbs:

- 3/4 cup of milk, whole
- 1 cup of peanut butter, smooth
- 2 x 11-oz. bags of morsels, butterscotch
- 2 tbsp. of water, boiling

For dipping

- Marshmallows
- Pretzels
- Cored, sliced apples

Instructions:

1. In a medium pan, warm milk on med. heat. Add butterscotch morsels. Stir while cooking for eight to 10 minutes, till smooth, then remove a pan from the heat.

2. Whisk in peanut butter till smooth. Add 2 tbsp. of boiling water and stir.

3. Transfer mixture to fondue pot with a candle under it. Use dippers to share.

Conclusion

This fondue cookbook has shown you...

How to use different ingredients to affect unique, warming tastes in many dipping dishes.

How can you include fondue recipes in your home repertoire?

You can...

- Make delicious melted cheese fondue, which you have probably heard of. It is just as tasty as it sounds.
- Cook broth for fondue, which is widely served for dinners and parties. You can find the ingredients in the grocery or frozen food sections of your local grocery store.
- Enjoy making the delectable seafood fondue dishes, with salmon and scallops. Fish is a mainstay in recipes year-round, and there are SO many ways to make it great.
- Make fondues using meat and veggies in your recipes. They take a delicious fondue base and make it into a meal.
- Make all kinds of desserts like strawberry shortcake fondue and chocolate fondues of all types, which will surely tempt anyone with a sweet tooth.

Enjoy these recipes with your family and friends!

About the Author

Allie Allen developed her passion for the culinary arts at the tender age of five when she would help her mother cook for their large family of 8. Even back then, her family knew this would be more than a hobby for the young Allie and when she graduated from high school, she applied to cooking school in London. It had always been a dream of the young chef to study with some of Europe's best and she made it happen by attending the Chef Academy of London.

After graduation, Allie decided to bring her skills back to North America and open up her own restaurant. After 10 successful years as head chef and owner, she decided to sell her business and pursue other career avenues. This monumental decision led Allie to her true calling, teaching. She also started to write e-books for her students to study at home for practice. She is now the proud author of several e-books and gives private and semi-private cooking lessons to a range of students at all levels of experience.

Stay tuned for more from this dynamic chef and teacher when she releases more informative e-books on cooking and baking in the near future. Her work is infused with stores and anecdotes you will love!

Author's Afterthoughts

I can't tell you how grateful I am that you decided to read my book. My most heartfelt thanks that you took time out of your life to choose my work and I hope you find benefit within these pages.

There are so many books available today that offer similar content so that makes it even more humbling that you decided to buying mine.

Tell me what you thought! I am eager to hear your opinion and ideas on what you read as are others who are looking for a good book to buy. Leave a review on Amazon.com so others can benefit from your wisdom!

With much thanks,

Allie Allen

Printed in Great Britain
by Amazon